U.S. Regions

# The Natural Environment of the Midwest

Blaine Wiseman

MEDIA ENHANCED BOOKS

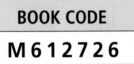

Go to **www.av2books.com**, and enter this book's unique code.

## BOOK CODE

**M 6 1 2 7 2 6**

**AV² by Weigl** brings you media enhanced books that support active learning.

AV² provides enriched content that supplements and complements this book. Weigl's AV² books strive to create inspired learning and engage young minds in a total learning experience.

## Your AV² Media Enhanced books come alive with...

**Audio**
Listen to sections of the book read aloud.

**Key Words**
Study vocabulary, and complete a matching word activity.

**Video**
Watch informative video clips.

**Quizzes**
Test your knowledge.

**Embedded Weblinks**
Gain additional information for research.

**Slide Show**
View images and captions, and prepare a presentation.

**Try This!**
Complete activities and hands-on experiments.

## ... and much, much more!

Published by AV² by Weigl
350 5th Avenue, 59th Floor
New York, NY 10118

Websites: www.av2books.com        www.weigl.com

Library of Congress Control Number: 2014942113

ISBN 978-1-4896-1226-7 (hardcover)
ISBN 978-1-4896-1227-4 (softcover)
ISBN 978-1-4896-1228-1 (single-user eBook)
ISBN 978-1-4896-1229-8 (multi-user eBook)

Printed in the United States of America in North Mankato, Minnesota
1 2 3 4 5 6 7 8 9  18 17 16 15 14

062014
WEP090514

Project Coordinator: Aaron Carr
Design: Mandy Christiansen

Every reasonable effort has been made to trace ownership and to obtain permission to reprint copyright material. The publishers would be pleased to have any errors or omissions brought to their attention so that they may be corrected in subsequent printings.

Weigl acknowledges Getty Images as its primary image supplier for this title.

# Contents

# U.S. Regions

**T**he United States has five major regions with different natural landforms, animals, plants, and **climate**. They are the Northeast, the Southeast, the Midwest, the Southwest, and the West. There are many differences within each region.

Washington

Montana

Oregon

Idaho

Wyoming

Nevada

Utah

Colorado

California

Arizona

New Mexico

Pacific Ocean

MEXICO

## Legend

- ■ West (11 states)
- ■ Southwest (5 states)
- □ Northeast (11 states)
- ■ Southeast (11 states)
- ■ Midwest (12 states)

**The Midwest is the only U.S. region that borders the other four regions and Canada.**

**The Midwest covers 821,733 square miles (2,128,277 square kilometers).**

Alaska

0    500 Miles
0    500 Kilometers

Hawai'i

0    100 Miles
0    100 Kilometers

CANADA

North
Dakota

Minnesota

Lake
Superior

New
Hampshire

Maine

Vermont

South
Dakota

Wisconsin

Lake
Huron

Lake Ontario

Massachusetts

Lake
Michigan

Michigan

New York

Rhode
Island

Nebraska

Iowa

Illinois

Lake Erie

Pennsylvania

New
Jersey

Connecticut

UNITED STATES

Indiana

Ohio

West
Virginia

Virginia

Delaware
Maryland

Kansas

Missouri

Kentucky

North Carolina

Oklahoma

Arkansas

Tennessee

South
Carolina

Atlantic
Ocean

Texas

Alabama

Georgia

Mississippi

N

Louisiana

Florida

0          250 Miles

Gulf of Mexico

0      250 Kilometers

# What Makes the Midwest?

**A** flat grassland region called the Great Plains covers the west-central United States and part of western Canada. The Great Plains makes up a major portion of the Midwest, but there is more to this region than flat ground. Fire, ice, and water have worked together to shape the land.

Over millions of years, volcanic activity helped create South Dakota's Black Hills and the High Plains of Nebraska and Kansas. **Glaciers** moved south down the North American continent, then retreated northward. They left plateaus, or raised areas of flat land, in what is now North Dakota. They also carved out areas that filled with water and became lakes. Meanwhile, rivers cut through the landscape all over the Midwest.

🖋 Black-tailed prairie dogs are grass-eating animals that live underground in burrows on the Midwest plains. They are named after the noise they make, which sounds like a dog's bark.

Four of the five Great Lakes are connected to the Midwest. Superior, Michigan, Huron, and Erie are some of the biggest lakes in the world. These bodies of water provide important **habitats** for the plants and animals of Michigan, Ohio, Indiana, Illinois, Wisconsin, and Minnesota.

The country's biggest rivers flow through the region, too. From Minnesota, which is sometimes called the "Land of 10,000 Lakes," the Mississippi River flows to the southern coast of the United States. Another major U.S. river, the Missouri, winds southeast across the plains before joining the Mississippi. These two rivers and their **tributaries** are an important source of water for the Midwest region.

# Major Landmarks of the Midwest

**T**he Midwest region is home to many natural wonders. Some of North America's oldest mountains are found in South Dakota. These mountains, called the Black Hills, were created 60 million years ago. Today, they cover 1.2 million acres (500,00 hectares) of land and tower 3,000 feet (900 meters) above the plains below. The Black Hills lie mostly in the Black Hills National Forest.

**South Dakota**, Jewel Cave
Beneath the Black Hills is the third-longest cave in the world, Jewel Cave. This cave is filled with crystal rock formations that sparkle under light. More than 160 miles (260 km) of the cave have been explored. People discover more of it every year.

🍃 The Black Hills are named for the dark pine trees that cover their slopes. Lakota Sioux Indians first called the area *Paha Sapa*, or "Black Hills."

**Michigan**, Sleeping
Bear Dunes
Lake Michigan is home to the
world's largest **freshwater**
sand dunes, or hills. Sleeping
Bear dunes rise 440 feet
(135 m) above the lake.

**Nebraska**, Scotts Bluff
On the banks of the Platte River, 800 feet
(245 m) of sandstone rise above the prairie,
or plains. Scotts **Bluff** is the remains of
land that covered the High Plains 33 million
years ago. When the land **eroded**, Scotts
Bluff and other rock formations, such as
Courthouse Rock and Jail Rock, survived.

**Nebraska**, Agate Fossil Beds
About 20 million years ago,
**mammals** that no longer exist
roamed the Midwest. Giant pigs
and animals called beardogs lived
in today's northwestern Nebraska.
Their remains can be seen in the
Agate **Fossil** Beds.

# South Dakota,
## Black Hills

Mount Rushmore
National Memorial,
carved in rock,
is part of the
Black Hills.

At 7,242 feet
(2,207 m) above
sea level, Harney
Peak is the
HIGHEST
point in South
Dakota.

In **1874**, gold was
discovered in the Black Hills.

# Major Biomes of the Midwest

**H**uman communities can be as large as a whole country or as small as a classroom. Plants and animals live in communities, too. The largest communities of plants and animals are called biomes. These are areas where the weather and other conditions allow certain types of living things to survive and grow. A grassland biome covers most of the Midwest.

## Mapping the Biomes of the Midwest

Use the map below and the information on the next page to answer the following questions.

1. How many states have only one biome?
2. Which states have more than one biome?
3. How many states have a **deciduous** forest biome?

## Grasslands

Climate: Dry, seasonal

Vegetation: Grasses

Temperature: -4° to 86° Fahrenheit

(-20° to 30° Celsius)

## Coniferous Forest

Climate: Seasonal

Vegetation: Evergreen trees

Temperature: -4° to 104°F

(-20° to 40°C)

## Deciduous Forest

Climate: Seasonal

Vegetation: Dense leafy trees, flowers

Temperature: -22° to 86°F

(-30° to 30°C)

In the Midwest, gray wolves hunt and feed on large animals such as deer, elk, and moose.

# Ecosystems of the Midwest

**E**cosystems are smaller communities within a biome. An ecosystem is made up of its natural environment, such as soil and water, as well as plants and animals. The parts of an ecosystem rely on one another to survive. The prairie is an example of a large ecosystem in the Midwest. It provides food and shelter to a variety of species, or types, of animals. It also supports the growth of many kinds of plants.

## Food for Thought

Living things need **nutrients** to survive. A food cycle is like a chain in which nutrients are passed from one living thing to another. A food cycle begins with plants, which make nutrients using sunlight and chemicals in the soil. These nutrients are passed on to an animal that eats the plants. When that plant-eating animal is eaten by a **predator**, the nutrients are passed on again. Then, the animal dies. In time, its body decomposes, or breaks down, adding chemicals to the soil. Plants then use these chemicals to make nutrients, and the cycle starts again.

## Food Cycle

Prairie wheatgrass begins the food cycle by making nutrients from the rich soil and bright sunshine.

Prairie dogs eat the wheatgrass and its seeds.

Black-footed ferrets hunt prairie dogs, gaining nutrients from the meat. They return the nutrients to the soil when they die.

## Eco Facts

Black-footed ferrets, burrowing owls, and barred tiger salamanders live in prairie dog burrows.

American bison swallow their food without chewing. Later, it comes back up from the stomach to be chewed and swallowed again.

*As many as one million earthworms can live in 1 acre (0.4 ha) of healthy soil.*

**Black-tailed prairie dogs live in large communities called towns. About**

## 400 million

**prairie dogs used to live in a single town.**

*Pronghorns are North America's* SPEEDIEST *mammal. They can run faster than 50 miles (80 km) per hour.*

# Major Rivers of the Midwest

**T**he Midwest is sometimes called the heart of the U.S. river system. The country's two largest rivers, the Mississippi and the Missouri, flow through this region. Many other rivers flow into and add water to them. All of these rivers create important habitats for a variety of plants and animals. One of these natural habitats is wetlands, or lowland areas covered with water.

**Minnesota**, Mississippi River
The Mississippi begins at Lake Itasca in Minnesota and flows 2,340 miles (3,766 km) to the Gulf of Mexico. Along the way, it collects water from the Ohio, Platte, and Wabash Rivers, as well as the Missouri and thousands of other streams and rivers.

**Missouri**, Missouri River
The second-longest river in North America is the 2,315-mile (3,726-km) Missouri. It begins in Montana and flows into the Mississippi River at St. Louis, Missouri.

**Nebraska**, Platte River
Flowing 990 miles (1,590 km) from Colorado across Nebraska, the Platte River empties into the Missouri River. It is an important source of water for farms. **Endangered** birds such as the whooping crane rely on its wetlands.

**Ohio**, Ohio River
The Ohio River flows 981 miles (1,579 km) from Pennsylvania to the Mississippi River in Illinois. It forms the border between Ohio and West Virginia. This river also serves as Kentucky's borders with Ohio, Indiana, and Illinois.

**Indiana**, Wabash River
For 529 miles (851 km), the muddy, slow-moving Wabash River flows through Indiana's plains. After forming the border of Indiana and Illinois for about 200 miles (320 km), the Wabash empties into the Ohio River.

# River Facts

**The Mississippi River drains, or collects water from, parts of 31 U.S. states and two Canadian provinces.**

The Missouri River is sometimes called "The BIG Muddy" or "The Muddy Mo" because it carries so much dirt.

**The Platte River is shallow. Its name comes from the French word *plat*, which means "flat."**

*Mussels have hard shells and live in water. Of the 80 mussel species that used to live in the Ohio River,* **only 50 are left.**

# Mammals of the Midwest

**T**he wide-open spaces of the Midwest are home to a large number of big and small mammals. From the huge American bison to the tiniest mouse, these animals rely on the grasslands to survive. Human activities cause problems for mammals such as the endangered black-footed ferret and Eastern cougar.

**Indiana,** Lynx

With a population around one million in nature, the lynx is North America's most common wildcat. However, it remains an endangered species.

**Kansas,** American Bison

The American Indians of the Great Plains hunted these animals, often called buffaloes. They used every part of the bison for food, clothing, shelter, and tools. When settlers arrived on the plains, millions of American bison were killed, and they almost died out in this area.

**North Dakota,** Nokota Horse

Nokota horses are related to horses that once roamed the plains of North Dakota in large numbers. Today, some Nokota horses live in Theodore Roosevelt National Park. People have been **breeding** them since the 1980s.

**Illinois, Michigan, Nebraska, and Ohio**, White-tailed Deer

The white-tailed deer has four stomachs. They help the animal eat and digest tough prairie grasses and other plants.

**South Dakota,** Coyote

Coyotes are members of the dog family that look like small wolves. They have adapted to life in many different ecosystems, including deserts, mountains, and plains.

**Missouri,** Missouri Mule

Missouri mules are stubborn farm animals that will protect other animals from predators such as bears and cougars. A mule is the **offspring** of a female horse and a male donkey.

**Minnesota,** Elk

Elk are a type of large deer. In 1935, elk were brought back to the natural habitats of Minnesota. Today, there are two elk herds in the state.

**Iowa,** White-tailed Jackrabbit

The white-tailed jackrabbit can run up to 35 miles (56 km) per hour, jump 20 feet (6 m), and swim to escape predators.

**Wisconsin,** Badger

The badger is a stocky, aggressive animal that is related to weasels and otters. It lives in burrows that it digs in the ground.

# Reptiles and Amphibians of the Midwest

**R**eptiles and amphibians are **cold-blooded** animals. Amphibians lay their eggs in or near water. Young amphibians, such as tadpoles, are called larvae. They are very different from adults. Larvae live in water and have **gills**, like fish. Then, as they change into adults, they grow lungs and begin to live on land. Salamanders, frogs, and toads are amphibians. Reptiles have **scales** for skin. They lay their eggs or give birth to babies on land. Turtles, lizards, snakes, and crocodiles are reptiles.

Today's amphibian species number 7,260.

There are 8,240 species of reptiles in the world.

## Official State Amphibians

**Illinois,** Eastern Tiger Salamander

Eastern tiger salamanders are a type of mole salamander. They use their short snouts to dig burrows. Adults spend most of their lives under logs and in wet soil.

**Kansas,** Barred Tiger Salamander

Barred tiger salamanders can measure more than 1 foot (0.3 m) long. They eat various insects, slugs, earthworms, and even small frogs.

**Missouri,** North American Bullfrog

The bullfrog is the largest North American frog. It makes a loud noise that can travel a long distance. Bullfrogs use their sharp talons, or claws, to hunt smaller animals.

# Official State Reptiles

**Illinois and Michigan,**
Painted Turtle

Painted turtles are named for the bright colors that mark their bodies and shells.

**Kansas,**
Ornate Box Turtle

The ornate box and the eastern box are the only two turtles of the Great Plains that spend almost all of their time on land.

**Missouri,**
Three-toed Box Turtle

Despite its name, the three-toed box turtle can have four toes on its back feet.

**Ohio,**
Northern Black Racer

A black racer tries to sound like a rattlesnake by shaking its tail in dried leaves. The noise scares predators away.

# Unofficial State Reptiles

**Iowa,**
Slender Glass Lizard

The slender glass lizard is not a snake species. It is a type of lizard with no legs. When caught by a predator, the lizard's tail will detach, allowing the animal can escape. The tail grows back later.

**Minnesota,**
Blanding's Turtle

Blanding's turtles can live for 70 years. The yellow-chinned turtles are an endangered species.

**Nebraska,**
Great Plains Rat Snake

The Great Plains rat snake hunts at night using a well-developed sense of smell. It feeds on rats, bats, and small birds.

# Birds of the Midwest

The Midwest provides a perfect habitat for many bird species. Foods such as seeds and insects are easy to find in the region's grasslands and wetlands. Plants, **rodents**, reptiles, amphibians, fish, and other birds are also food sources for the birds of the Midwest. However, many birds have lost some of their habitat as the number of people and settlements in the Midwest has grown. The whooping crane, interior least tern, and Kirtland's warbler are examples of endangered birds in the Midwest.

**South Dakota,** Chinese Ring-necked Pheasant
South Dakota's state bird was brought from China in 1898. Its meat was highly valued in states outside the Midwest.

Hunters in the United States take more than 20 million mourning doves every year.

Birds of the Midwest that hunt other birds include hawks and owls.

Mammals, birds, and even fish hunt loons.

**Minnesota,** Common Loon
Loons spend most of their time in water. They build nests on the edge of a river or lake. Minnesota's lakes offer a perfect habitat for loons. In the summer, their calls echo across their habitat.

**Iowa and Nebraska,** Eastern Goldfinch
The eastern, or American, goldfinch feeds on the seeds of flowers and weeds such as dandelions. These birds are **herbivores** and eat insects only by accident.

### Missouri, Eastern Bluebird

Female eastern bluebirds build nests and care for baby birds. A male brings nest materials to a female only as part of a mating practice.

### Wisconsin, Mourning Dove

The mourning dove is the official peace symbol of Wisconsin. The bird's call sounds similar to crying, or mourning.

### Illinois, Indiana, and Ohio, Northern Cardinal

The northern cardinal began moving north into Midwestern habitats in the 20th century. As the climate has continued to become warmer in recent years, this cardinal keeps moving to locations farther north.

Some American Indian groups in the Midwest perform traditional prairie-chicken dances.

*Every year, during their long trip through the Midwest, whooping cranes stop to rest and eat at wetlands.*

Kirtland's warblers live only among jack pine trees of a certain height. When the trees grow taller than about 13 feet (4 m), the birds look for new nesting sites.

### Kansas and North Dakota, Western Meadowlark

Western meadowlarks eat bugs that live in the soil of grasslands, as well as grain and seeds. The female nests on the ground in prairie or other grassland habitat.

### Michigan, American Robin

American robins are one of North America's most common birds. After rain, they often dig in the wet soil for earthworms to eat.

# Plants of the Midwest

The trees, shrubs, grasses, and wildflowers that grow in the Midwest are as varied as the land, climate, and animals. The plants in this region serve many purposes. Plants are part of the food cycle. They also shade, give homes to, and protect the region's insects, birds, rodents, and mammals.

### Illinois
**Big bluestem** is a type of grass that can grow 10 feet (3 m) tall. It is also called turkey feet or beard grass because of how it looks when it blooms.

### Indiana
**Peonies** can be pink, red, white, or yellow. They are popular in gardens and flower bouquets.

### Iowa
**Wild rose** can be seen in all parts of Iowa. This flower has been growing in North America for 35 million years.

The head of a sunflower is actually as many as 2,000 flowers joined together.

Prairie grasses act like anchors for the soil, keeping the wind from blowing it away.

### Kansas
**Sunflowers** can grow to 15 feet (4.6 m) tall. They produce about 1,000 seeds each. As the Sun moves across the sky, sunflowers turn to face the sunlight.

### Michigan
**Dwarf lake iris** is a vivid blue flower about 2 inches (5 centimeters) in height. It grows in only a few places near Great Lakes beaches.

### Minnesota
**Pink and white lady's slipper** plants grow as tall as 4 feet (1.2 m) high. They can live as long as 50 years. White-tailed deer often feed on this colorful flower.

## Missouri
**White hawthorn** flowers grow on a plant that can be 20 feet (6 m) tall. Hawthorns are related to roses and apples.

## Nebraska
**Goldenrod** blooms in July. Its bright yellow flowers can be seen all over Nebraska. Goldenrod is a perennial. That means it grows back year after year from the same **bulb**.

## North Dakota
**Western wheatgrass** grows naturally all over North Dakota. It is a hearty grass that can grow well even in times of low rainfall. Farmers use it for feeding their cattle.

The flower of the dwarf lake iris is only 1.5 inches (4 cm) wide.

There are about 150 species of goldenrod in the world.

## Ohio
**White trillium** flowers are also known as snow trillium or wake trillium. As the white flowers age, they turn pink or purple.

## South Dakota
**Pasque flower** is a poisonous plant that grows throughout South Dakota. It is also known as the May Day flower and the Easter flower.

## Wisconsin
**Wood violet** is a food source for many animals. People use the leaves for salads, candies, and jellies.

# Challenges Facing the Midwest

**N**atural areas in the Midwest are facing many different challenges. Over the past 150 years, millions of people have moved into the region. Cities, towns, and roads have been built. Farms raising crops and **livestock** cover the prairie. Crops and animals grown in the Midwest are needed to feed people around the world. Most of North America's prairie is now used for farming. This changing landscape affects the Midwest's natural habitats, animal life, and people.

Today, almost 1,300 American bison roam the prairies and hills of Custer State Park in South Dakota.

# Human Impact

On land across the Midwest, crops such as corn and soybeans have replaced **native** grasses. Some animals that depended on these grasses have died out. Fertilizers, which help crops grow, can also put chemicals into the soil that harm animal life. Rain may wash these chemicals into rivers and streams. This can be harmful to fish and other animal life in and near these water sources.

Grasslands and wetlands are easily damaged by some types of human activity. If these areas are destroyed, ecosystems may be lost forever. Some people and groups are working to make sure that natural ecosystems in the Midwest are protected.

Corn crops cover 13.1 million acres (5.3 million ha) of land in Iowa alone.

# American Bison

Before European settlers arrived in North America, there were as many as 60 million bison in the region. Settlements and large-scale hunting reduced the number of bison in the United States to only a few hundred by the 1880s.

**THOUSANDS** of bison were killed each day by hunters on the Great Plains in the 1870s.

Today, about **30,000** American bison live in public and private herds and **400,000** are raised as livestock.

Bison are the heaviest land mammals in North America.

# Endangered Species Spotlight

In the 20th century, a loss of habitat, disease, and hunting killed about 98 percent of the prairie dog population. The situation was even worse for the black-footed ferret, which feeds on prairie dogs. By 1986, only 18 black-footed ferrets remained, and none of them lived in nature. After the U.S. Fish and Wildlife Service began a **breeding program**, these animals are beginning to return to the Midwest. Today, about 500 black-footed ferrets exist in nature, and another 300 live in breeding programs.

The leafy prairie-clover can grow well on the plains of the Midwest. This plant needs plenty of rainfall in the spring and fall, as well as large amounts of sunshine in the summer. Those weather conditions occur on the plains in most years. As people move into natural areas, however, they create roads, communities, and farms where clover used to grow.

The black-footed ferret is North America's only native ferret.

The endangered interior least tern is the smallest member of the gull and tern family. It measures about 9 inches (23 cm) in length.

During the summer, interior least terns live on river **sandbars** and banks in the Midwest. These small birds dig shallow holes in the sand to lay their eggs. Dams built on some rivers have changed their water levels and flooded sandbars. This has reduced the population of terns by removing the habitat they need to lay eggs and raise their young.

## Get Involved

The number of black-footed ferrets has been growing since they were **reintroduced** in nature. However, the species remains endangered. Habitat loss and disease are problems for ferrets. Diseases that can take the lives of ferrets have been brought into their habitats as a result of human activities. The Black-Footed Ferret Recovery Program is one of the efforts now under way to help ferrets survive and increase in number, both in nature and in breeding programs.

You can get involved in efforts to save the black-footed ferret. The website of the Black-Footed Ferret Recovery Program provides detailed information about these ferrets, including how they live, their history in the Midwest, and programs that support them. The website also lists ways that people can help this species to survive.

For more information, visit the Black-Footed Ferret Recovery Program at www.blackfootedferret.org/how-to-help.

# Activity

**A** keystone is the large center block at the top of a stone arch. It is a very important piece of the arch because it holds all the other stones in place. Prairie dogs are called a "keystone species." They have been given this title because they are so important to their ecosystems.

In fact, prairie dogs build ecosystems. They give other species a food source, as well as a place to live. Their digging **aerates** the soil and their droppings fertilize it. As a result, prairie dogs help grass and flowers grow. This gives herbivores plenty of food to eat. When plant-eating animals thrive in an ecosystem, the **carnivores** that hunt them are plentiful as well. Besides the prairie dogs themselves, many other animals live in prairie dog burrows. In all, about 150 other species rely on prairie dogs.

Today, there may be about 10 to 20 million prairie dogs on the plains. In the past, there were more than one billion.

# Make a Food Web

Use this book, and research on the internet, to create a food web for the prairie.

1. Make a list of animals that live in or near prairie dog burrows.

2. Divide your list into two. The first list is titled "Carnivores." Put the meat-eating animals in this list. The other list is called "Herbivores." Put the plant-eating animals in this list.

3. Make a food web with grass at the center. Draw lines between the species to show which animals eat others. The arrow shows the transfer of energy, in the form of food, from one animal to the other.

4. Now, make another food web, but remove the prairie dog.

5. How does removing the prairie dog affect the other species? Write down your thoughts and share them with your classmates and family.

## Sample Food Web

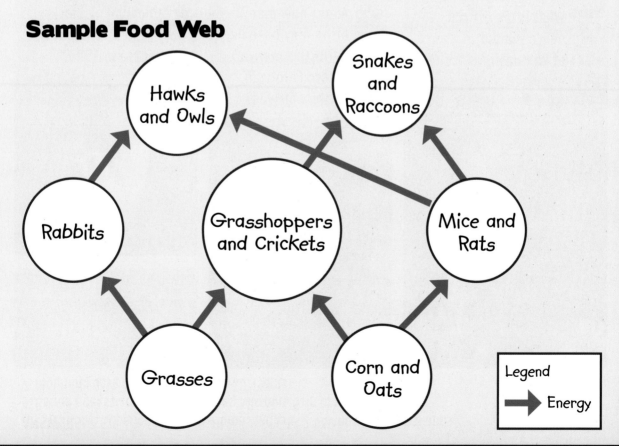

# Quiz

**1** Which Great Lakes are connected to the Midwest?

**2** Which state is known as the "Land of 10,000 Lakes"?

**3** What is the largest biome of the Midwest?

**4** What amphibian is known to live in prairie dog burrows?

**5** In what city do the Missouri and Mississippi Rivers meet?

**6** Where do amphibians lay their eggs?

**7** What is the official peace symbol of Wisconsin?

**8** About how many bison may have lived in North America before European settlers arrived?

**9** How many black-footed ferrets were there in 1986?

**10** What is the main type of food that herbivores eat?

**ANSWERS: 1.** Superior, Michigan, Huron, and Erie **2.** Minnesota **3.** Grasslands **4.** Barred tiger salamander **5.** St. Louis, Missouri. **6.** In or near water **7.** Mourning dove **8.** 60 million **9.** 18 **10.** Plants

# Key Words

**aerates:** supplies with air

**bluff:** a high, steep bank or cliff

**breeding:** creating new members of a species

**breeding program:** the planned breeding and raising of animal species that are at risk of dying out in their natural habitats

**bulb:** a rounded underground plant part from which a new plant can grow

**carnivores:** animals that feed mostly on other animals

**climate:** a region's usual weather conditions

**cold-blooded:** having a body temperature that changes with the environment's temperature

**deciduous:** losing leaves each winter

**endangered:** at risk of no longer surviving on Earth or in a particular region

**eroded:** washed away, by water or wind

**fossil:** prehistoric remains preserved in rock

**freshwater:** water that is not salty

**gills:** organs that fish and amphibians use to breathe underwater

**glaciers:** giant slabs of ice that move slowly down a slope or across land over time

**habitats:** the places where an animal or plant naturally lives

**herbivores:** animals that feed mainly on plants

**livestock:** farm animals

**mammals:** animals that have hair or fur and drink milk from their mother

**native:** originating or growing in a certain place

**nutrients:** substances that living things need to survive and grow

**offspring:** the young of a person, animal, or plant

**predator:** an animal that hunts other animals for food

**reintroduced:** when animals raised in breeding programs are put back in their natural habitat to live

**rodents:** types of animals with sharp front teeth, such as mice, rats, squirrels, and beavers

**sandbars:** raised areas of sand that are just above the water level in a river or other body of water

**scales:** small, stiff plates that form the outer covering of some types of animals

**tributaries:** small rivers that flow into larger rivers

# Index

# Log on to www.av2books.com

AV² by Weigl brings you media enhanced books that support active learning. Go to www.av2books.com, and enter the special code found on page 2 of this book. You will gain access to enriched and enhanced content that supplements and complements this book. Content includes video, audio, weblinks, quizzes, a slide show, and activities.

## AV² Online Navigation

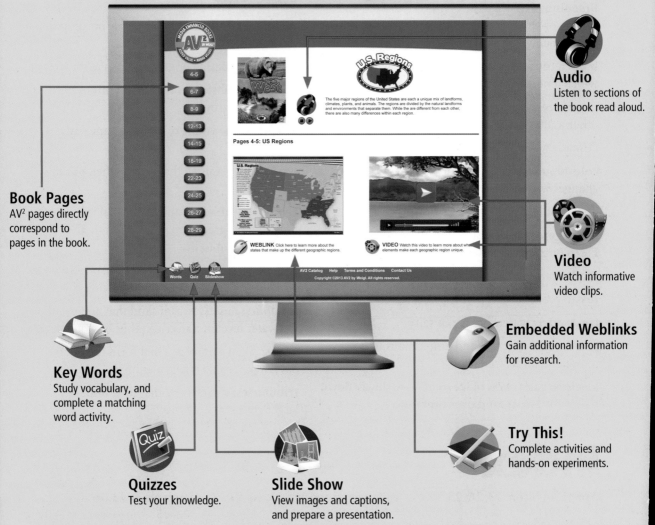

**Audio**
Listen to sections of the book read aloud.

**Book Pages**
AV² pages directly correspond to pages in the book.

**Video**
Watch informative video clips.

**Key Words**
Study vocabulary, and complete a matching word activity.

**Embedded Weblinks**
Gain additional information for research.

**Try This!**
Complete activities and hands-on experiments.

**Quizzes**
Test your knowledge.

**Slide Show**
View images and captions, and prepare a presentation.

AV² was built to bridge the gap between print and digital. We encourage you to tell us what you like and what you want to see in the future.

## Sign up to be an AV² Ambassador at www.av2books.com/ambassador.

Due to the dynamic nature of the Internet, some of the URLs and activities provided as part of AV² by Weigl may have changed or ceased to exist. AV² by Weigl accepts no responsibility for any such changes. All media enhanced books are regularly monitored to update addresses and sites in a timely manner. Contact AV² by Weigl at 1-866-649-3445 or av2books@weigl.com with any questions, comments, or feedback.